BLENDER 4.3

Guidebook

A Step-by-Step User Manual to Master 3D Modeling, Animation and Texturing

Benson Paul

Disclaimer and Terms of Use

The author, publisher, and contributors have made every effort to compile this work carefully and accurately. However, no guarantees are provided regarding the accuracy, applicability, or completeness of the information contained within. The content is for informational purposes only. If you choose to apply any concepts from this book, you do so at your own risk and responsibility.

Printed in the United State of America

Table of Contents

CHAPTER ONE

Getting Started

Blender 4.3 is the most recent gigantic discharge of the strong open-source 3D modeler, presently smooth and effective, loaded with luxurious highlights and planned for enabling specialists, artists, amusement engineers, visual impacts experts, or genuine novices. It moreover comprises basic enhancements to fortify the existing major functionalities.

Key Highlights

Comprehensive Toolset:

1.Bender envelopes a tremendous cluster of instrument necessities beneath one roof-modeling, chiseling, texturing, enlivening, rendering, and compositing, among others.

2.Its work consistently partners 2D and 3D workflow, empowering the creation of profoundly complex cross breed ventures.

Improved Rendering Motors:

1.Cycles: Extended back for made strides rendering execution within the setting of caustics and to handle more complex lighting scenarios in Blender's physically based way tracer.

2. EEVEE: The real-time rendered sports imperative overhauls, such as volumetric lighting, delicate shadows, and accessible progressed impacts for see and speedier emphases.

3. Modeling and fundamental visualization are best done with Workbench that has too been set up for effectiveness.

Geometry Hubs Improvements:

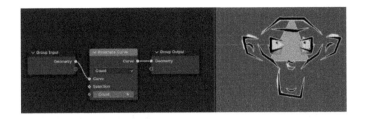

1.Blender 4.3 presents modern hubs for diffusing, misshaping, and procedural workflows, enabling the craftsman to create practically point by point situations and vivified objects exceptionally effectively.

2. Execution and convenience enhancements render procedural modeling much speedier and more instinctive.

Movement and Fixing Overhauls:

1. These incorporate upgraded liveliness apparatuses with way better highlights within the Chart Editor, progressed insertion modes, as well as new fixing devices to form a more productive character setup.

2. Movement Ways and the NLA Editor have both been made strides to encourage more exact and effective workflow.

Material science and Reenactments:

1) Definition of liquid, smoke, fire, and dress for more complex reenactments has been extended.

2) Other modern solvers will be competent of giving comes about, computation times, and accuracy that are much made strides, particularly when large-scale recreations are conducted.

Texturing and Chiseling Instruments:

1.Greatly progress chiseling forms with included brushes and patched up flow.

2.Similarly, surface portray is much more effective and flexible than some time recently, with modern mixing modes for the method.

Client Interface and Ease of use: Patching up of the controls conclusion client interface progressed ease of use.

Who Is Blender 4.3 For?

Blender 4.3 caters to an intimidatingly expansive range of individuals:

Experts: The producers, diversion makers, illustrators, and visual impacts specialists can utilize the devices of Blender to create a really high-quality generation.

Understudies and Specialists: With its free and open source nature, Blender is really a really great learning device for apprentices investigating the 3D craftsmanship.

Studios: Blender will near up very pleasantly with any proficient workflow, being able to coordinated into pipelines through open measures and its Python API.

Reasons to Select Blender 4.3:

- Free and Open Source. Totally free to utilize. Open permit empowers adjustment and redistribution.

- Dynamic Community. This buzzing offer assistance is truly an universal community creating instructional exercises, plug-ins, and assets.
- Cutting-edge Innovation. Upgrades are nourishing into Blender frequently so that its employments at the beat of the line in 3D plan and activity.

Installing Blender 4.3

1.Step-by-Step Foundation Coordinate Download Blender:

1. Visit the official Blender location:

https://www.blender.org.

2.Go to the Download zone and select Blender 4.3 for your working system (Windows, macOS, or Linux). Present Blender:

1. Windows: Download the .msi installer and run it. At that point take after the on-screen illuminating to add up to the foundation.

2.macOS: Download the .dmg record, open it, and drag Blender into the Applications organizer.

3. Linux: Download the tarball, remove it, and run the executable record. On the other hand, utilize your bundle chief on the off chance that Blender 4.3 is available in your distribution's stores.
Step-by-Step Coordinate for Foundation:

Download Blender:

1. Visit the official Blender location, which can be found at: https://www.blender.org.

2. By and by, go to the Download range and select Blender 4.3 for your working system, whether it is Windows, macOS, or Linux.

Present Blender:

1. For Windows, download the .msi installer and execute it. At that point, take after the on-screen illuminating to wrap up the foundation.

2. For macOS, download the .dmg record, alacrity it, and drag Blender into the Applications organizer. 3.

For Linux, download the tarball, empty it, and run the executable record. Or utilize your bundle chief in case Blender 4.3 is open in your distribution's stores.

Designing Blender 4.3

Beginning Setup:

Set Slants:

1.Go to Modify > Slants (or Blender > Slants on macOS).

2.Configure fundamental inclinations counting: The character or slant a gadget ought to tune in to (e.g., selecting the mouse button to a left/right one).

3.Keymap changes. Physical accommodation notice (this can be exceptionally critical to encourage a smooth execution on the off chance that Cycles or EEVEE endeavoring the issue).

Save Startup Record: Adjust your workspace and properties, at that point continue to the Record > Defaults > Save Startup Record to store your setup.

Add-ons:

1.Turn on critical expansion devices inside the Slants > Add-ons in thevbrowsecu, circle. Spin-off contraptions such as "Observe Wrangler," "Rigify," or "BlenderKit" may be the settling of great contemplations.

Surrounded Courses of action:

Scratch down the compatibility list for:

1.Make beyond any doubt the GPU drivers are up to date for successful multitasking in rendering.

2.Select the rendering gadgets to utilize in Slants > System (Cycles) such as CPU, GPU, or cross breed rendering execution modes. Adhere to the following lines over leading with 3-overall.

CHAPTER TWO

User Interface

The Blender 4.3 interface is laid out for viability and flexibility, catering to both disciples and specialists. With a exceedingly customizable organize and common devices, the UI ensures steady course and openness over all its highlights.

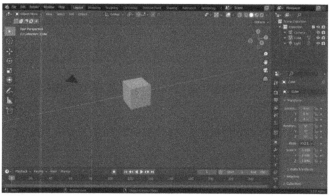

Window Framework

Blender features a exceptionally adaptable window framework that permits one to set up one's workspace in a non-overlapping way.

Workspaces: Predefined formats best suited for particular assignments:

Modeling, Chiseling, Liveliness, Shading, and Rendering. Making, renaming, sparing of custom workspaces is conceivable.

Editor Sorts: Each window in Blender can be set to a certain sort of editor; this could be the 3D Viewport, Shader Editor, Chart Editor, or UV Editor. Alter editor sorts utilizing the pull-down menu within the top-left corner of each editor window.

Part and Joining Windows:

- To part a window: Drag from corner of window to part it into two.
- To connect windows: Drag one window onto the beat of another to connect them Range CONTROL
- To extend or contract regions: Drag on the borders
- Save a unused format: Record > Defaults > Spare Startup Record.

Keymap

Keymapping in Blender is broad and there to optimize workflow with hotkeys.

- Default Keymap: Efficient default format with numerous commonly utilized apparatuses mapped to instinctive keys such as G for Snatch, S for Scale, R for Turn. Both cleared out- and right-clicking is backed (client inclination).

- Custom Keymap: Alter >> Inclinations >> Keymap Rummage around for any activity, at that point utilize the additionally to dole out your possess key. Keymaps can be traded and imported for consistency on distinctive systems.

If the client has worked in any other 3D programs, there's an interchange Blender keymap more like other industry standards.

UI Components

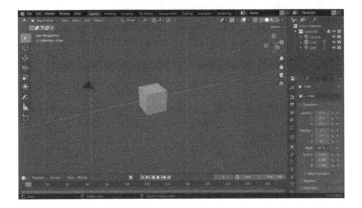

Blender's interface is composed of different UI components, each serving a particular reason.

Headers: Found at the best or foot of each editor, they give get to menus and devices important to the current editor.

Boards:

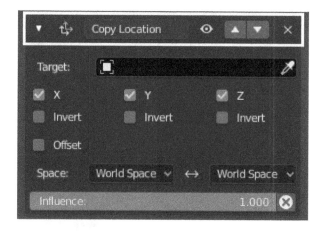

- Contain gathered settings, shown in vertical formats.
- Expand and collapse boards by clicking their headers.

Sidebar:

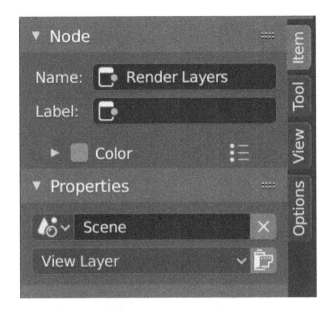

- Toggle the sidebar in most editors with N.
- Provides speedy get to to properties and tool-specific choices.

Setting Menus: Access context-sensitive choices with a right-click or W (depending on the keymap).

Toolbars: Access tools and settings on the left-hand side of the 3D Viewport or other editors by squeezing T.

Tools & Operators

Blender's apparatuses and administrators streamline the creation and altering handle over different workflows.

Device Framework:

- Located within the toolbar, on the cleared out side of the 3D Viewport
- Commonly utilized fundamental apparatuses incorporate: Select, Move, Pivot, Scale, and Change.

Administrator Look: Press F3 or Spacebar depending on your keymap and get to any menu thing from this look bar

Alter Final Operation: After performing an operation, its settings can be changed from the bottom-left corner of the 3D Viewport or from the Re-try Final board (F9).

Modifiers and Limitations: These apparatuses, accessible within the Properties Editor, naturally perform dreary errands and include procedural adaptability to workflows.

Nodes

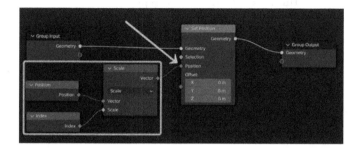

Blender's node-based framework permits clients to form complex materials, recreations, and impacts procedurally.

Sorts of Hub Editors:

- Shader Editor: For making materials utilizing PBR workflows or custom shading impacts.
- Geometry Hub Editor: For procedural modeling and instancing.
- Compositor: For post-processing rendered pictures.
- Texture Hub Editor: For procedural surface creation.
- Hub Interface: Nodes are spoken to as boxes associated by noodles (lines). Inputs on the

cleared out and yields on the correct define information stream.

Hub Bunches: Combine different hubs into a single reusable gather. Enhance seclusion and organization in complex setups.

Modern Highlights in Blender 4.3

- Additional hubs for diffusing, misshapening, and quality administration.
- Improved execution for expansive hub trees and more natural hub connecting.

CHAPTER THREE

Editors

Blender's interface is built around measured editors that cater to particular assignments. Each editor can be arranged autonomously, which makes for a really customizable workflow. Below is an diagram of the foremost critical editors in Blender 4.3.

3D Viewport

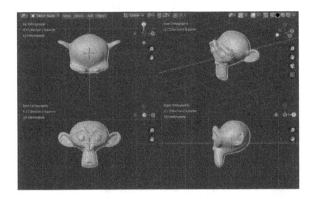

The 3D Viewport is the central workspace where interaction with 3D scenes happens, supporting modeling, chiseling, activity, and more.

Key Highlights:

- Navigation: Circle, container, and zoom utilizing the mouse or alternate route keys (MMB, Move + MMB, Scroll Wheel).
- Modes: With the different protest, alter, shape, surface paint, among other modes.
- Overlays: This will turn on/off a few distinctive highlights on-screen (e.g. lattice, gizmos) through its sub-menu alternatives.

- Shading: Shading choices (Wireframe, Strong, Fabric See, Rendered) are gotten to through the top-right corner.

Picture Editor

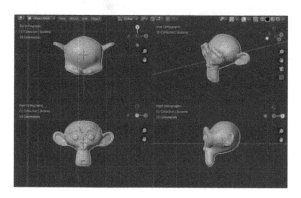

Picture Editor A window for showing and controlling picture surfaces, renders and UV maps.

Key Highlights:

- Image Portray: Paint the surfaces straightforwardly in Blender with portray apparatuses.
- Render Comes about: It shows the rendered pictures, which incorporate composited yields.

- UV Altering: Altering UVs and visualization of the connected surfaces on 3D models.

UV Editor

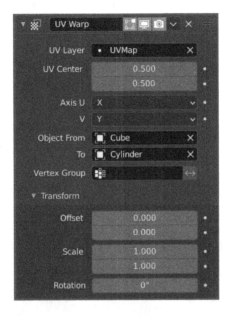

The UV Editor centers on unfurling and altering of UV maps that control how textures will be mapped to 3D surfaces.

Key Features:

- UV Unwrapping: Consequently or physically unwrap models for surface mapping.
- UV Instruments: Fasten, adjust, scale, and control UV islands for ideal surface formats.
- Sync Determination: Work intuitiveness between the UV Editor and 3D Viewport.

Shader Editor

It's conceivable to form complex materials interior the Shader Editor in a node-based workflow.

Key Highlights:

- Node-Based Material Creation: Utilizing hubs to make procedural surfaces, PBR materials, and much more.
- Shader Sorts: Underpins fabric shader, world shader and light shader.
- Real-Time Sneak peaks: Visualize changes within the Material Preview or Rendered mode within the 3D Viewport.

Compositor

The Compositor could be a exceptionally capable instrument for post-processing rendered pictures and recordings.

Key Highlights:

- Node-Based Workflow: Include color evaluating, glare, and depth-of-field impacts utilizing hubs.
- Integration: Coordinated render passes, such as shadows, reflections, and encompassing impediment, for more control.
- Real-Time Upgrades: Composited changes are seen instantly within the Picture Editor.

Content Editor

Text Editor could be a basic, general-purpose editor which can be utilized to type in scripts or make notes interior Blender.

Key Highlights:

Notes: Store project-related notes or enlightening.

Syntax Highlighting: Composing and investigating scripts is simpler.

Video Sequencer

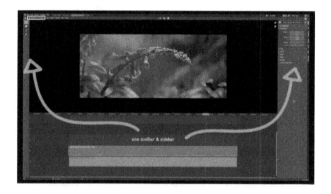

The Video Sequencer is used for fundamental video altering and movement sequencing.

Key Highlights:

- Video Altering: Cut, trim, and after that orchestrate video clips on a timeline.

- Effects: Include moves, color adjustments, and other impacts.

- Audio Back: Sound tracks to complement the video film.

- Timeline: Center editor for movement timing. It shows keyframes and permits playback control.

- Chart Editor: Alter F-Curves for fine control over movement addition and facilitating.

- Dope Sheet: Visualize and control keyframes over different objects or activities in a compact arrange.

- Geometry Hub Editor: Make procedural models and impacts utilizing the hub framework.

- Properties Editor: Get to settings for objects, materials, modifiers, and the by and large scene.

- Outliner: Oversee the chain of command and organization of objects in your scene.

- Record Browser: Browse and oversee records to consequence, send out, and connect.

CHAPTER FOUR

Scenes and Objects in Blender 4.3

Blender organizes 3D ventures into Scenes:

Self-contained records containing all objects, activity, lights, cameras, and everything else in a extend. This is often a neighborly way of collecting Scenes in information squares that manage indeed superior extend organization for more complex ventures.

Scenes

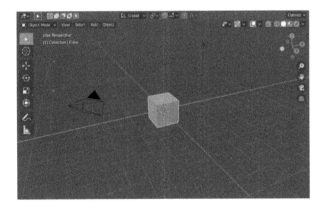

A Scene in Blender may well be a workspace that characterizes the environment, settings, and components for a particular parcel of your amplify.

You'll have diverse scenes interior one Blender document, which grants you to work on differing parts of a expand in independent sessions.

1. Key Highlights of Scenes

Independent Settings:

- Each scene can have its claim render settings, world environment, and address organization.
- This makes it straightforward to work on assortments of a amplify, such as particular camera focuses, lighting setups, or exuberance courses of action.

Shared Data: Objects, materials, and other data can be shared over scenes utilizing Associated Data. Changes made to a shared component will be reflected in all scenes that utilize it.

Scene Trading:

1. To switch between scenes, utilize the dropdown menu at the beat of Blender's interface.

2. Scene Organization

Counting Scenes: Make advanced scene by clicking Incorporate > Scene from the Data Editor's dropdown menu.

New: Modern clear scene

- Duplicate Settings: Same as over but copies the current scene's render and world settings
- Full Duplicate: Full copy of the scene with all objects and settings
- Connected Copy: A unused scene with associated objects and data
- Deleting Scenes: To eradicate an unused scene right-click the scene inside the dropdown menu and select Eradicate.
- Interfacing and Including: To solidify assets or components from other Blender records into your as of presently open scene, utilize Record > Interface or Record > Include.

Scene Properties

The Scene Properties tab of the Properties Editor offers a infers to modify many basic settings for the as of presently open scene:

Render Settings: Assurance, Framerate, Testing, Development Darken, and more.

Outline Amplify: Characterize the start and conclusion diagrams for action playback and rendering.

Objects

Objects are the elemental building pieces of any scene in Blender. Each protest talks to an substance inside the 3D world, such as a work, light, camera, or cleanse.

1. Dissent Sorts

Work: Talks to 3D geometry made of vertices, edges, and faces (e.g., a 3d shape or a circle).

Light: Lights up the scene; joins point, sun, spot, and run lights.

Camera: Characterizes the point of view for rendering the scene.

Curve/Surface/Text: Way, decorating shape, or 3D substance.

Armature: A settle for character development

Cleanse: Imperceptible accomplice dissent utilized for organization, child raising, or reference

Volume, Metaball, Grease Pencil, among others.

2. Challenge Changes

Translation: to move any dissent with G key

Transformation: to rotate any dissent with the R key

Scale: to change an object's degree with S key

Controllers: gizmos in 3D Viewport for visual changes.

3. Address Properties

These settings, gotten to through the Properties Editor, are object-specific and consolidate qualities of zone, materials, confinements, modifiers, and various more.

Collections

Collections bunch objects together for organization and scene organization. They are versatile, allowing both a visual pecking arrange and valuable utilize in rendering and perceivability control.

1. Making and Directing Collections

Create a Collection: Right-click inside the Outliner and select Unused Collection or press M to move chosen objects into a advanced collection.

Hierarchy: Collections can be settled to create a organized chain of command.

Renaming: Double-click the collection title inside the Outliner to rename it.

2. Perceivability and Abrogates

• Stow absent Collections: The images for the eye, camera, and viewport flipping of perceivability inside the Outliner.

• Abrogates: To form changes to because it were certain objects or collections from a data piece without changing the primary.

3. Interfacing and Including Collections

• Collections can be included or associated from other Blender records for reuse of assets and collaboration on ventures.

Layers

See Layers allow you to organize the porousness and rendering of objects for different parts of your amplify. They're especially important for rendering scenes with various passes or making varieties without replicating the scene.

1. Reason of See Layers

Create diverse render passes (e.g., apportioned closer see and establishment objects).

Simplify complex scenes by flipping the penetrability of objects and collections.

2. Orchestrating See Layers

Incorporate Cutting edge See Layer: Press Utilize Unused within the Show Layer Properties tab.

Alter Show Layer Settings: Specify which objects or collections are unmistakable in which show layer. Exclude collections or objects by clicking on the checkbox symbols within the Outliner.

3. Render Passes

Sorts of Passes: Render person passes such as shadows, reflections, diffuse, or circuitous lighting. These can be utilized within the Compositor for post-processing.

Enable Passes: Setup render passes within the See Layer Properties tab beneath the Passes.

Workflow Integration

Organizing with Collections: Gather comparative objects for occurrence, lights props, and characters to create working in your scene simpler. One can utilize settled collections for dynamic organization

Utilizing See Layers for Rendering

- In a measured workflow, dole out collections to see layers to render.
- Keeping the components into the layers optimizes the render times.
- Consolidating Objects and Collections inside Outliner
- Utilize the Outliner to naturally oversee objects, choices and see layers.

CHAPTER FIVE

Modeling

Meshes

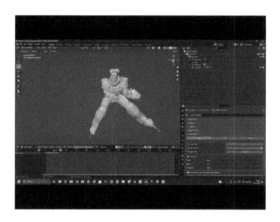

Systems are the preeminent adaptable modeling objects in Blender, comprising of vertices, edges, and faces.

1. Work Modifying

Edit Mode: Gotten to with Tab, gives disobedient for altering work geometry.

Selection Gadgets: Vertex (1), Edge (2), and Go up against (3) modes for centered on modifies. Box, Circle, and Rope assurance disobedient.

Essential Operations

- Expel (E):Make unused geometry by pulling out faces.
- Inset (I): Incorporate humbler faces insides chosen faces.
- Incline (Ctrl + B): Smooth corners and edges.
- Circle Cut (Ctrl + R): Incorporate edge circles for superior control.

2. Work Primitives

Get to basic shapes like 3d shapes, circles, barrels, and planes by implies of Incorporate > Work. B Twists are utilized for making smooth, spilling shapes and ways.

1. Twist Sorts

- Bezier: Control centers with editable handles for smooth twists.
- NURBS: Non-Uniform Sound B-Splines, best for logically correct shapes.

2. Twist Changing

- Control handles to modify recede and stream.
- Convert to work for progress modifying by implies of Challenge > Alter over To > Work.

3. Applications

Path development, custom beveling, and profile time.

Surfaces

A bit like bends, be that as it may differing, surfaces are utilized inside the creation of smooth tireless 3D surfaces.

NURBS Surfaces: Best for Mechanical and car modeling. Editable in Change Mode, for more unmistakable exactness in forming.

Metaballs

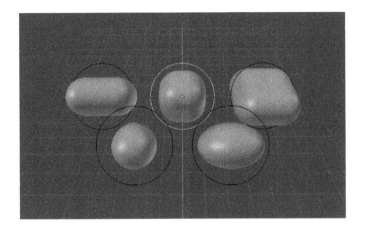

Metaballs Normal shapes that combine when in close closeness.

Usage:

- Add metaballs by implies of Incorporate > Metaball.
- Adjust assurance and blending inside the Properties Editor.

Applications: Modeling fluid-like structures, hypothetical craftsmanship, and base shapes for chiseling.

Substance

Substance objects allow for the creation of 3D typography.

1. Counting Substance: Add substance through Incorporate > Substance.

2. Modifying Substance

Edit Mode: Alter the substance substance.

Object Properties: Modify printed fashion, course of action, scattering, and more.

3. Alter

Alter over substance to a work for custom shaping through Dissent > Alter over To > Work.

Modifiers

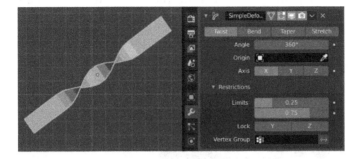

Modifiers apply non-destructive changes to objects.

1.Common Modifiers

- Subdivision Surface: Smoothens geometry by subdividing faces.
- Cluster: Copies objects in a direct or circular design.
- Mirror: Reflects geometry over and hub.
- Boolean:
- Combines or subtracts geometry from objects.

2.Modifier Stack

Combine different modifiers for complex impacts. Modify modifiers within the stack to alter their arrange of impact.

Geometry Hubs

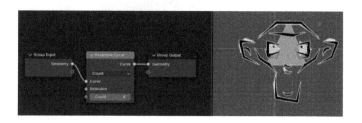

Geometry Center points allow procedural modeling by meddle center points in a visual editor.

1. Node-Based Workflow

- Incorporate a Geometry Center points modifier to your dissent.
- Utilize the Geometry Center Editor to form custom center setups.

Applications

Procedural Scenes. Particle impacts. Reusable assets.

Changes

Changes are principal for arranging and shaping objects.

1. Alter Sorts

- Move (G): Translate objects or geometry.
- Rotate (R): Turn around a turn point.
- Scale (S): Change assess generally.

2. Snapping and Exactness

- Use Move for correct changes.
- Enable snapping (magnet image) for altering objects.

3. Comparing Modifying

Enable with O in Modify Mode to change over geometry with a falloff impact.

CHAPTER SIX

Sculpting & Painting

Sculpting

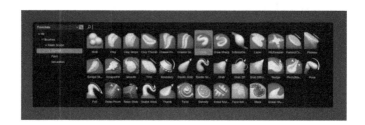

Chiseling may be energetic, brush-based workflow for altering work geometry, to some degree associated to working with advanced clay.

1.Sculpting Essentials Shape Mode: Get to by means of the mode dropdown within the 3D Viewport or with Ctrl + Tab.

Brushes:

1.Blender has a few brushes for smoothing, drawing, expanding, and squeezing among other assignments.
2.Modify brushes within the Brush Properties panel.

Symmetry: Activate symmetry choices (X, Y, Z tomahawks) within the Symmetry settings to create alters reflected.

Key Highlights

Energetic Topology (Dyntopo): Programmed subdivision of work whereas chiseling gives better subtle elements on the off chance that required. It is gotten to through Dynamic Apparatus Settings.

Multi-resolution Modifier

- Adds more subdivision levels to permit for non-destructive chiseling.
- Great for high-resolution specifying and keeping a low-poly base work intaglio.

Voxel Remeshing: It re-meshes the work into equally conveyed geometry, which is extraordinary for keeping smooth topology when chiseling.

3. Utilize Cases

- Character Chiseling: Natural shapes incorporate faces, animals, and humanoid models.
- Specifying: Include subtle elements like wrinkles, scales, and surfaces.
- Shape Investigation: Rapidly sketch over and emphasize shapes and shapes.

Surface Portray

Surface Portray empowers you to paint straightforwardly onto a 3D demonstrate or a 2D picture for detailed surfaces, designs, and colors.

Fundamental Surface Portray

1.Texture Paint Essentials

Surface Paint Mode: Available from the mode dropdown within the 3D Viewport or the Picture Editor. Within the 3D Viewport, paint is done directly onto the 3D show. In the Picture Editor, work on UV-unwrapped surfaces.

Brushes: Diverse brushes, such as Draw, Spread, Clone, and Veil, can be utilized for nitty gritty surface work. Customize settings like quality, measure, and surface covers.

2. Setup for Surface Portray

- Texture Openings: Characterize the surfaces beneath Fabric Properties, for illustration, base color, harshness, etc.
- UV Mapping: The show ought to be UV-unwrapped for setting the right surface.
- Image Surfaces: Make and allot picture surfaces within the Picture Editor.

3. Key Highlights

- Mask: Decide regions to paint or secure with vertex bunches or custom covers.
- Stencil Portray: Picture stencils to put designs
- Multi-Channel Painting: Paint over different fabric channels, color, ordinary, harshness, all at the same time.

4. Surface Portray Workflows

- Hand-Painted Surfaces: Paint stylized surfaces directly onto the demonstrate.
- Photo Projection: Venture photo-realistic surfaces onto models utilizing picture stencils.
- Consistent Surfaces: Consistent tileable textures painting in 2D.

Vertex Portray

Vertex Portray may be a methodology of depict the colors clearly onto the vertices of a demonstrate. Since this technique stores colors as parcel of the work data, it is light and resolution-independent.

Basic Vertex Depict

1. Vertex Paint Mode: Get to through the mode dropdown inside the 3D Viewport or with Ctrl + Tab.

Brushes: Utilize instruments like Draw, Spread, and Obscure to apply or change vertex colors. Customize brush properties-strength, degree, falloff-in the Energetic Apparatus Settings.

Color Organization: Set base colors and blending modes inside the Brush Properties board.

2. Applications of Vertex Depict

- Artistic Impacts: Include hand-painted focuses of intrigued and points for stylized models.
- Masking and Modifiers: Utilize vertex colors as cloak for materials, geometry centers, or modifiers.
- Previsualization: Rapidly visualize color plans and plans without requiring UV maps or surfaces.

3. Tips for Practical Vertex Depict

- High Vertex Thickness: Guarantee your work has adequate geometry to hold point by point color information.
- Combine with Materials: Utilize the Quality center inside the Shader Editor to apply vertex colors in materials.

Weight Portray

Weight Portray Weight values are relegated to the vertices of a work, most regularly for controlling the impact of bones, material science, or other modifiers.

1.Weight Portray

- Essentials Weight Paint Mode: Get to through the mode dropdown within the 3D Viewport or with Ctrl + Tab. Brushes:
- Paint weights (values from to 1) utilizing apparatuses like Include, Subtract, Obscure, and Normal. Alter brush quality and falloff for exact control.
- Visualization: Weights show up as a slope of colors extending from blue-0 influence-to red-1 impact.

2. Applications of Weight Portray

- Rigging and Cleaning: Perform weight portray to dole out weights to vertices for bone impacts in character activity.

- Physics Reenactments: Indicate impact zones of cloth, delicate body, or vertex bunch modifiers.
- Vertex Bunch Control: Utilize weight-painted vertex bunches for procedural impacts, such as molecule outflow or distortion.

3. Key Highlights

- Automatic Weights: Join an armature to a work utilizing Parent with Programmed Weights for a beginning point.
- Normalize Weights: Make beyond any doubt weights add up to 1 to induce smooth miss happening by empowering Auto Normalize within the Instrument Settings.
- Lock Bunches: Bolt certain vertex bunches to maintain a strategic distance from inadvertent altering.

Vertex Painting vs. Weight Painting

Feature	Vertex Painting	Weight Painting
Purpose	Adds visual color data to vertices.	Assigns influence values for deformations or effects.
Data Type	Vertex Colors	Vertex Weights (0–1 values).
Applications	Artistic effects, texture masks, material blending.	Rigging, physics, procedural modifiers.
Visualization	Color painted directly on the model.	Heatmap gradient (blue to red).

CHAPTER SEVEN

Grease Pencil

Drawing with Grease Pencil

Blender's Grease Pencil instrument permits you to draw specifically within the 3D viewport, making 2D drawings or total 2D liveliness inside a 3D environment.

1. Grease Pencil Nuts and bolts

Grease Pencil Question: To begin drawing, include a Grease Pencil question by selecting Incorporate > Grease Pencil > Clear or Stroke. A Grease Pencil question comprises of layers, outlines, and strokes, where each layer holds 2D strokes.

2. Draw Modes

Draw Mode: Enter Draw Mode to start drawing strokes specifically within the 3D Viewport. The Stroke, Fill, and Shape brushes do diverse employments.

Instruments

- Pencil Instrument: Draw freehand strokes.
- Line Apparatus: Draw straight lines or bends.

- Rectangle Device: Draw filled rectangular shapes
- Circle Device: Make circular shapes or covers.
- Polyline Apparatus: Draw a few associated lines.
- Bend Device: Draw smooth bends with mobile control focuses.

3. Brush Settings

Opens the setting of brush settings - estimate, quality dispersing, and bend falloff interior the Instrument Settings board.

Surface: Flip between the brush being compelled to a 3D surface or free inside 2D space.

4. Layers and Diagrams

- Layers: The possibility to work in isolated layers is exceptionally valuable to draw, ink, and color.
- Frames: Make traces for setting up your drawings in sets of movement. Utilize key outlines to invigorate your strokes.

5. Tablet Back

Grease Pencil expands drawing tablets, which are able to provide weight affectability to line weight, tone, and stroke smoothness.

6.Drawing on a 3D Surface

You'll be able to draw specifically onto a 3D surface by enabling Stroke Arrangement within the Apparatus Settings. This permits you to utilize the surface geometry as a direct for your drawings.

Altering Grease Pencil

After having made your strokes, you'll be able assist alter and invigorate them utilizing the Alter Mode together with other apparatuses in Blender.

1. Alter Mode

- Edit Mode could be a mode where you'll be able alter Grease Pencil strokes by selecting and changing them.

- Select person focuses, strokes, or whole layers.

- Move

- G, Turn

- R, or Scale

- S strokes as required.

Geometry Altering: Change over strokes to bends or alter their thickness, murkiness, and fabric properties. Subdivide strokes to add more focuses and refine their shape.

2. Shape Mode

- Sculpt Mode lets you detail your Grease Pencil strokes in a more creative way.
- The chiseling brushes will alter the volume and shape of your strokes, supportive in 2D character drawing and movement.

3. Utilizing the Grease Pencil Modifier

- Subdivision Surface or Remesh modifiers let you control stroke detail and execution optimization.
- Modifiers can be utilized to quicken, fashion, or alter the by and large stroke thickness and smoothing.

4. Liveliness and Keyframes

- Grease Pencil bolsters 2D liveliness with conventional frame-by-frame methods.

- Keyframe Strokes: Make different keyframes with distinctive drawings, and Blender will add the outlines in between.
- Use Dope Sheet and Chart Editor to oversee and alter your activity keyframes, a bit like with 3D objects.

5. Altering Strokes within the 3D Viewport

- Strokes can be moved in 3D space and hence setting up 2D activity in a 3D scene is clear.
- Move, Turn, and Scale strokes within the 3D Viewport as portion of setting up the activity.
- Perceivability: Control which of the Grease Pencil objects/ layers are unmistakable and which can be rendered.

6. Fill and Stroke Editing

- Stroke styling: thickness and color are altered through alteration of materials.
- Fill: include color between strokes to form strong shapes.

7. Child rearing & Limitations

- Grease Pencil objects can be parented to other 3D objects for more progressed activity.
- Use limitations to control the movement or position of the strokes relative to 3D objects.

Applications of Grease Pencil

- 2D Liveliness: Make 2D activities inside the 3D environment of Blender. You'll quicken everything from straightforward shapes to complex characters.
- Storyboarding: Drawing thoughts and unpleasant movement groupings in a storyboard organize.
- Movement Design: Create animated 2D components that can connected with 3D objects, useful for movement design ventures.
- Concept Craftsmanship: Rapidly outline and outline design ideas on paper; it's simple to imagine concepts in 3D space.

Modifiers for Grease Pencil

Modifiers in Grease Pencil are comparative to those for work objects but adjusted to work with 2D strokes and shapes. They allow procedural changes and alters without touching the first information.

1. Sorts of Grease Pencil Modifiers

Transform Modifiers:

- Disentangle: This reduces the number of focuses in strokes. It is valuable for execution optimization or to make rearranged adaptations of drawings.
- Subdivision: Smooths the strokes by including more focuses.
- Grid: Misshape strokes by a cross section protest in complex ways.

Generate Modifiers:

- Construct: Makes an movement of drawing a stroke continuously.
- Cluster: Cluster strokes along an hub.

- Occurrence: Occasions the strokes with changes.
- Reflect: Mirror strokes along indicated tomahawks for symmetry.

Deform Modifiers:

- Snare: Snares strokes to an outside protest for coordinate control.
- Shrinkwrap: Ventures strokes onto a 3D surface
- Counterbalanced: Move stroke positions agreeing to an counterbalanced figure

Fashion Modifiers:

- Thickness: It'll alter the in general thickness of strokes.
- Mistiness: Stroke straightforwardness for energetic visual impacts is modified.
- Tint: It applies a color tint to strokes or fills.

2. Utilizing Modifiers

- Add modifiers within the Modifiers Tab beneath the Properties Editor.
- Stack different modifiers for layered impacts.
- Apply Modifier to create changes changeless on the off chance that fundamental.

Impacts for Grease Pencil

Impacts incorporate stylization to Grease Pencil objects, which enables visual changes such as clouding, glimmering, or mangling strokes.

1. Sorts of Impacts Stylization Impacts:

- Shine: Incorporates a sparkling format to strokes for neon or highlighted impacts.
- Wave: Makes wavy mutilations in strokes, profitable for reproducing improvement like water or wind. Shadow:
- Incorporates a shadow to strokes, giving a sense of significance.

Mutilation Impacts:

- Clamor: Self-assertively mangles strokes, making nervous or unrefined appearances.
- Swell: A swell from a center point; awesome for impacts or shockwaves.
- Twirl: Turns strokes around a central point for a swirl-like affect.

Dynamic Impacts:

- Opacity: Stroke straightforwardness vivified over time.
- Obscure: Plumes stroke edges for a smooth or phenomenal appearance.

2. Applying and Customizing Impacts

- To incorporate impacts, go to the Modifiers Tab, at that point to the Segment called Impacts.
- Play with parameters like quality, appraise, and color to realize your needed result.
- Effects are non-destructive and can be stacked or reordered. Workflow Integration Combining Modifiers and Impacts:

- Utilize Build Modifier with Glimmer Affect to enliven sparkling strokes being drawn. Combine Reflect Modifier and Wave Affect for symmetrical be that as it may lively plans. Activity:
- Energize modifier or affect properties for enthusiastic visual moves.
- Illustration: Enliven the Obscurity Affect for obscuring strokes in or out.

CHAPTER EIGTH

Shading

Materials

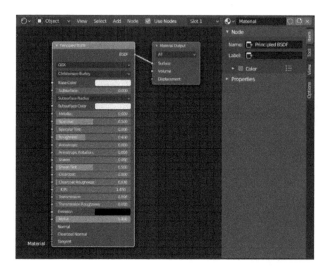

Materials will characterize the surface properties of objects, counting color, reflectivity, unpleasantness, and straightforwardness.

1. Fabric Creation

- Open the Fabric Properties tab within the Properties Editor.
- Click Modern to include a fabric to the chosen protest.

- Adjust Base Color, Harshness, Metallic, and Emanation.

2. Fabric Sorts

- Principled BSDF-A general-purpose shader for nearly anything, counting diffuse, shiny, and subsurface diffusing in one hub.
- Emission-Objects radiating light, such as a screen or light.
- Glass BSDF: Usually utilized for straightforward and refractive surfaces, such as glass or water.
- Volume Materials: These are materials utilized to render volumetric effects-smoke, haze, or clouds.

3. Doling out Materials

Materials can be relegated to an protest as a entirety or to parts utilizing Fabric Spaces.

In work objects, materials are alloted to person faces in Alter Mode.

Shader Hubs

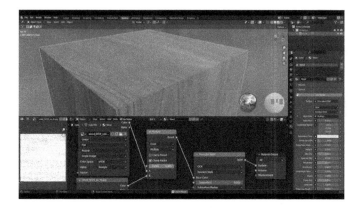

The Shader Editor engages the help fine-tuning of materials with the utilize of center points. Each center talks to a work that ought to be executed, expanding from surface mapping to logical operations.

1. Diagram of Shader Center points

- Open the Shader Editor from the Editors Menu or by flipping the foot window inside the default organize.
- Each Center joins to other center points by implies of input and surrender connections, making a orchestrate of the material's definition.

2. Common Shader Center points

- Principled BSDF: A physically-based, all-purpose shader.
- Diffuse BSDF: For clear, non-reflective surfaces.
- Glossy BSDF: For brilliantly materials, like metal or cleaned surfaces.
- Mix Shader: Combines more than one shader, engaging the creation of mixed impacts.
- Emission: Licenses a surface to radiate light.

3. Workflow Tips

- Use Color Slant center points for more correct modifications in points or move impacts.
- Insert Math or Vector Math centers for controlling numeric or directional data.
- Mix Shader and Direct BSDF can be combined for to some degree clear materials.

Surface Hubs

Surfaces incorporate surface detail, such as plans, bumps, or movements.

1.Surface Sorts

- Picture Surfaces: Pictures stacked from outside for point by point or photorealistic surfaces.
- Procedural Surfaces: These are made insides Blender, cases join Clamor, Voronoi, Musgrave.

2.Surface Mapping

The Surface Organize and Mapping centers control how the surface wanders onto the surface.

Common mapping sorts:

UV: Diagram surfaces concurring to custom UVs. Generated: Modified mapping associated concurring to geometry.

Protest: Based on dissent space encourages.

Surface Modifications

Bump Center: Reenacts surface variations from the norm by changing over grayscale surfaces into bump maps.

Relocation Center: Physically misshapes the work with a surface.

Typical Diagram Center: Incorporates fine surface detail utilizing ordinary maps.

Combining Shading Components

1. Hub Gathering: Bunch complicated hub setups into reusable Hub Bunches.

Case: Fair bunch the combination of surface mixing, commotion, and uprooting into one for seclusion.

2. Layered Materials: Blend shaders together to attain multi-material property combinations; for case, glass surface with tidy.

Utilize a veil or surface outline to decide where each fabric ought to be connected.

3. Lighting and Shading: Materials associated with scene lighting, so empower EEVEE or Cycles for a real-time/ray-traced shading see.

Alter light properties, among others, like escalated, color, and shadow settings to upgrade the fabric impacts.

Applications and Utilize Cases

- Authenticity: Using procedural and picture surfaces along side the principled shader.

- Stylized Craftsmanship: Emanation and striking colors for NPR purposes.

- Energetic Impacts: Quicken shader properties, like color moves or surface changes.

CHAPTER NINE

Lighting

Light Objects

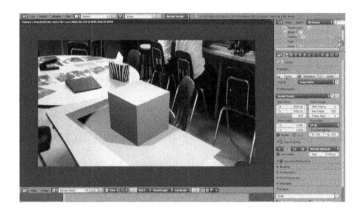

Light objects are sources of brightening that can be included into a scene for the reenactment of real-world lightings.

1. Sorts of Light Objects

Point Light: Will transmit light in all headings from one source, such as a bulb would.

Properties:

Control: intensified of the light.

Sweep: evaluated measure of a light source will influence the subtlety/shadow of light.

Sun Light: Imitating of sunshine traveling in parallel

2. Working Lights Objects

Alter light properties within the Properties Editor's Light Properties tab. Utilize Viewport Shading with EEVEE or Cycles to urge prompt input on how the changes in lighting will appear. Move and pivot light objects to realize the specified impacts.

World Foundation

The world foundation makes environment lighting reenacting the sky, open air conditions, or a few put.

1. Making a World Foundation

In the Properties Editor switch to the World Properties tab.

- Add a foundation with a Foundation shader.
- Color: The base color of the environment light.

- Quality: Quality of the natural lighting.

2. HDRI Lighting

- HDRI Tall Energetic Run Picture surfaces donate genuine comes about in environmental lighting.
- In Shader Editor include a modern hub for an Environment Surface.
- Stack an HDRI picture to supply practical light and reflections.
- Alter revolution and strength for best impact.

3. Sky Surface

- Utilize the Sky Surface for physically exact skies.
- Alter parameters like Turbidity (cloudiness) and Sun Rise.

Light Tests

Light tests are utilized to capture and recreate roundabout lighting, reflections, and shadows, improving authenticity in your scenes.

1. Light Test Sorts

- Reflection Cubemap: Capture the reflection from including objects to be utilized by materials.
- Irradiance Volume: Captures and reenacts circuitous lighting for a volumetric extend.
- Reflection Plane: Reenacts the reflection on level surfaces, like mirrors or water.

2. Counting Light Tests

- To incorporate light tests, investigate to Incorporate > Light Test.
- Purposely put tests in a scene to capture lighting or reflections.
- Altering test properties can be depleted the Challenge Data Properties tab:

Assurance: Controls the detail of the captured data.

Impact Locale: This states the volume or expand it impacts the test.

3. Warming Light Tests

- To warm the light test information, utilize the underhanded lighting tab underneath the properties of Render.
- Baking permits for optimized execution in conjunction with suitable light impacts on the scene.

Lighting Workflow Tips

- For fulfilling balanced lighting, utilize the combination of HDRI World Establishment at the side Light Objects.
- Using Light Test in Indoor Scenes makes strides reflections and indirect lighting of objects.
- Change light settings in real-time utilizing EEVEE or Cycles render engines.
- Light Bunches: The credibility to restrict specific lighting impacts for correct control.

CHAPTER TEN

Rendering

Render Settings

Render settings decide how your scene is handled and visualized by Blender's render motors.

1. Render Motors

- Cycles: A physically-based way following motor for practical renders.
- Suitable for high-quality stills and liveliness.
- Supports CPU and GPU rendering.

EEVEE:

- A real-time render motor for quick sneak peaks and stylized visuals.
- Ideal for liveliness, NPR (Non-Photorealistic Rendering), and ventures requiring speedy criticism.

Workbench:

- Designed for viewport rendering, with fundamental shading and overlays.
- Used for format sneak peaks or specialized outlines.

2. Testing

- Sets the sum of beams Blender calculates for each pixel, which controls render quality versus commotion.
- Render Tests: Test tally for last renders
- Viewport Tests: Test number for 3D Viewport see
- Denoising: Smooths out render commotion. Works in render and viewport.

3. Light Ways (Cycles as it were)

Controls how light interatomic within the scene:

- Max Bounces: Set greatest number of bounces that will happen between light reflection/refractions

- Straightforwardness Bounces: Alter most extreme number of bounces on straightforward surfaces

4. Execution Settings

- Tiles: No Part the render into tiles for handling.
- Larger tiles are superior for GPU rendering; littler tiles, for CPUs.
- Adaptive Inspecting: Consequently, changes tests per pixel based on commotion.
- Persistent Information: Speedier rendering by reusing information between outlines.

5. Volumes

- Step Rate: Directs the adjust of detail versus execution in volumetric rendering.
- Tile Measure: Permits changing the tile estimate of volumes for optimization.

6. Movement Obscure

Adds obscure to moving objects for reasonable liveliness.

Settings:

- Shade: Controls the length of the movement obscure.
- Steps: More exact movement obscure but with a few execution exchange off.

Yield Alternatives

Yield alternatives characterize the organize, determination, and goal of your rendered records.

1.Resolution

Set determination in Yield Properties beneath the Measurements board.

- Determination X/Y: Width and stature in pixels.
- Percentage: Determination as a rate of the base values.

Common settings:

HD:

- 1920x1080. 4K:

- 3840x2160.

2.Frame Rate

Set outlines per moment (FPS) for activity. Common presets are 24 FPS (cinematic), 30 FPS (standard), 60 FPS for high-motion scenes.

3. Yield Organize

Select record designs for rendered pictures or movements.

Picture:

- PNG: Lossless arrange with straightforwardness bolster.
- JPEG: Compressed arrange for littler record sizes.
- EXR: Tall energetic run for compositing.

Liveliness:

- FFmpeg Video: For video records with codecs like H.264.
- AVI: Uncompressed video for tall quality.

4. Record Yield Settings

Set yield area within the Yield Properties board.

- Record Way: Indicate the envelope where renders will be spared.
- Record Naming: Blender naturally adds outline numbers to liveliness records.

5. Compression

- Compression sum for at slightest PNG and JPEG record sorts.
- In recordings, alter the bitrate and codec settings within the Encoding board.

6. Render Passes

- Split the render into isolated passes for post-processing.
- This is accessible beneath the See Layer Properties tab.

Common Workflow Tips

- Test Renders: Do little resolutions or moo tests for quick sneak peaks.
- Batch Rendering: Use command-line rendering for enormous movements.
- Output to EXR: Save as EXR-for most extreme adaptability in a compositing workflow.
- Render Stamps: Include metadata to the picture, like outline number or render time for following.

Free-form

Free-form Free-form is an NPR instrument inside Blender that will draw stylized lines over your render.

1.Enabling Free-form: Open the Render Properties tab. Beneath Free-form check the checkbox to turn on Free-form line rendering.

2.Freestyle Settings:

- Line Thickness: Beneath the Free-form Line Fashion settings, set worldwide line thickness in pixels.

- Line Color: Underline color 3. Free-form Line Sorts:
- Line styles are set within the View Layer Properties within the Free-form board.

Edge Sorts:

- Silhouette: It outlines the shape of a question.
- Border: It shows where the protest closes and the foundation starts.
- Crease: It makes sharp edges discernible.
- Material Boundaries: It draws lines where diverse materials meet.
- Confront Smoothness: Changes how lines take after along a surface's ebb and flow.

4. Line Fashion Modifiers

Modifiers can be included to improve line styles:

- Thickness: Change line thickness along its length.
- Straightforwardness: Mistiness to blur out lines.

- Geometry: Include wavy or jumpy impacts with Spine Stretcher or Perlin Clamor.

5. Workflow Tips

- Utilize Free-form for activity, specialized drawings, or comic-style visuals.
- Combine Free-form with Compositor Hubs to combine rendered lines with scene components.

Color Administration

Color administration guarantees that your renders have the proper tone and color commitment for unmistakable show up contraptions or inventive enthusiastically.

1. Color Administration Framework OpenColorIO - Blender businesses OCIO for correct color organization, found beneath the Render Properties tab inside the Color Organization range.

2. View Change Manages how Blender maps scene-referred colors to display-referred colors Filmic. Default setting when doing photorealistic

rendering Can handle tall enthusiastic increase (HDR) lighting effortlessly

Standard: Employments a coordinate color profile. Less complicated or legacy ventures are appropriate. Crude: Does not show colors with tone mapping.

CHAPTER ELEVEN

Compositing

Compositor Editor

The Compositor Editor is the workspace merely utilize to form and oversee hub systems for compositing.

1. Getting to the Compositor

- Open the Compositor workspace or alter an editor to be the Compositor Editor.
- At the beat of the editor, empower Utilize Hubs to flip on the hub tree.

2. Key Highlights

- Node Organize: The compositing workflow is totally node-based. Hubs speak to activities, impacts, or information acting upon and changing the input picture.
- Backdrop: Gives a foundation see of the composited result within the hub editor.

Empower the background by clicking the Scenery choice within the header.

- Render Layers Input: The Render Layers hub is utilized to input rendered pictures from the dynamic see layer.

Composite Hubs

Composite hubs are the building squares of the compositing workflow. They prepare and modify the render and outside inputs.

1. Input Hubs

Render Layers:

- Brings within the render result from the scene.
- Can get to particular passes like Diffuse, Reflexive, Surrounding Impediment, and more.

Image: Import outside pictures or arrangements for compositing.

2. Yield Hubs

- Composite: The last yield that Blender processes and spares.
- Viewer: Used for visualizing middle of the road comes about amid compositing. Displays yield within the UV/Image Editor.
- File Yield: Saves particular parts of the composite to disk.

3. Color Hubs

Modify colors in your scene:

- RGB Bends: Adjust individual color channels employing a bend.
- Hue Immersion Esteem: Adjust the tone, immersion, and brightness of an picture.
- Color Adjust: Fine-tune shadows, midtones, and highlights.
- Gamma: Alter mid-tone brightness.

4. Channel Nodes

Apply visual impacts to the picture:

- Blur: Mellow points of interest utilizing different obscure sorts like Gaussian or Quick Gaussian.
- Glare: Include focal point flares, streaks, or shine impacts.
- Sharpen: Improve edges for a crisper picture.

5. Vector Hubs

Work with movement or profundity information:

- Normal: Process ordinary pass information for impacts like relighting.
- Z Combine: Combine profundity data from different inputs.
- Vector Obscure: Include movement obscure employing a vector pass.

6. Matte Hubs

Create and adjust covers:

- Keying: Extract green or blue screens for chroma key impacts.

- Luminance Key: Cover areas based on brightness levels.
- Mask: Utilize covers made within the Veil Editor.

7. Converter Hubs

Transform or prepare information:

- Set Alpha: Combine an picture with an alpha channel.
- Combine/Separate RGBA: Control person color channels.
- Math: Perform scientific operations on values or information.

8. Gather Hubs

- Combine different hubs into a single bunch for less demanding administration.
- Select hubs and press Ctrl+G to form a gather.
- Edit the bunch by squeezing Tab whereas interior it.

Workflow Tips for Compositing

Use Render Passes: Enable particular passes (e.g., Diffuse, Gleaming, Shadow) within the See Layer Properties to isolated render components for point by point compositing.

- Preview Changes: Use the Watcher hub to check middle of the road comes about as you construct the composite.
- Optimize Execution: Reduce picture determination amid testing to speed up compositing.
- Save Hub Trees: Save commonly utilized hub setups as Hub Bunches for reuse in other ventures.

Keying

Keying - it implies, to disconnect and expel the parcels of the picture with particular or specific color extend. It's as a rule done with green screen or blue screen effects.

1.Keying Workflow

- Include Keying Hub: Within the Compositor Editor, press Move + A, go to Matte, and tap on Keying.
- Input the Picture: Interface your source image-green screen video or photo-to the input of the Keying hub.
- Set the Key Color: Eyedropper within the Key Color property to select between green or blue foundation color.

Params Alter

Clip Black/White: Refine the key by altering the dark and white clip values to refine parts of the picture.

Despill Figure: Diminishes the undesirable color spilling from the foundation onto the subject.

2. Progressed Keying Strategies

- Chroma Key: Chroma Key Hub permits more nitty gritty color ranges.
- Resistance Sliders permits for fine-tuning.

- Erode/Expand Hub: Apply an Erode/Expand hub after keying to recgrease or develop the cover range. Obscure the Edges:
- Include Obscure hub to mollify spiked edges around the keyed-out range.

3.Compositing with Other Hubs:

- Utilize the Alpha Over hub to composite the yield of the Keying hub over a modern foundation. Utilize the Watcher Hub to see the alpha channel and check the result of the keying.

Concealing

Veiling empowers you to choose regions of an picture to composite or alter by one means or another. Essential Veiling

1.Creating Covers

Veil Editor: Open the workspace, Veil Editor, or by opening the UV/Image Editor set to mode

Drawing a Veil:

- Press the Add Cover Layer button.
- Ctrl + Cleared out Press to put focuses, making the cover shape.
- Modify handle for bends and edges. Feathering:
- Add plume focuses to smooth the mask's edges for mixing.
- Cover Layers: Make different veil layers for complex concealing.

2. Compositing with Veils: Within the Compositor Editor, add a Veil hub. Within the settings of the hub, select your cover from the dropdown menu. Interface the cover with other hubs, such as:

- Blend: This will combine the veil with images for specific mixing.
- Obscure: To make feathered edges for covers, permitting for smooth moves.
- Set Alpha: This will set the cover as an alpha channel for straightforwardness.

3. Quickening Veils

- Keyframes: Energize cover focuses within the Veil Editor by empowering auto keying or embeddings keyframes physically.
- Child rearing to Objects: Within the 3D Viewport, parent the cover to a moving protest to powerfully cover it.

Keying and Veiling Tips

Watcher Hub: Utilize it to check the alpha channel for cleanliness of the cover or keying prepare.

Combine Veils: Utilize the utilize of various cover layers with Boolean operations to incorporate progressed highlights like Include, Subtract, Meet.

Render Passes: Render particular passes like Question File or Cryptomatte for exact veiling.

CHAPTER THIRTEEN

Physics

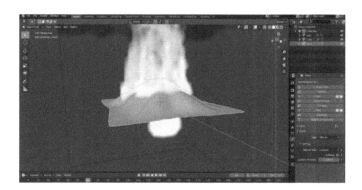

Rigid Body

Unyielding Body Fabric science mimics solid objects that do not mutilate in the midst of collisions or instinctive.

1. Counting Unbendable Body Fabric science
2. Select an address.

3. Go to the Fabric science Properties tab and press Unbendable Body.

Key Settings

- Dynamic: Objects that respond to powers and collisions. Inactive:
- Stationary objects that other objects associated with.
- Mass: Characterizes the weight of the object-affects development.
- Shape: Decides the collision bounds, such as Box, Circle, Work.
- Elements: Alter contact, bounciness, and damping for viable development.

Impediments

Utilize Inflexible Body Limitations to put through objects.

Outlines: Rotate, Settled, Point, Slider.

Delicate Body

Sensitive Body material science reproduces versatile, deformable objects like flexible or stick.

1.Including Sensitive: Body Fabric science. Select an address. Within the Fabric science Properties tap Sensitive Body.

2.Key Settings Objective: Grapple centers to protect the object's shape.

Edges: Control the adaptability and solidness of the address. **Collision:** Empower collisions with other objects and self-collisions.

3.Workflow Tips Utilize Vertex Bunches to characterize locales for fragile body behavior.

Increase reenactment quality by refining the Solver and Steps Per Second.

Cloth

Fragile Body fabric science reproduces versatile, impressive objects like versatile or stick.

1.Including Fragile Body Fabric science. Select an challenge. Within the Fabric science Properties tap Sensitive Body.

2.Key Settings

Goal: Stay centers to protect the object's shape.

Edges: Control the adaptability and immovability of the address.

Collision: Empower collisions with other objects and self-collisions.

3. Workflow Tips

Utilize Vertex Bunches to characterize zones for sensitive body behavior. Increase reenactment quality by refining the Solver and Steps Per Moment.

Liquid

Liquid recreations make practical water, fluid, or other fluid-like impacts.

Adding Fluid Material science: Select a space object (usually a 3d shape). Within the Material science Properties tap Liquid.

Key Settings Sort

- Space: the region in which the liquid recreation happens.
- Stream: characterizes liquid source - Fluid, Smoke
- Determination: Higher determination gives way better comes about but will take more time to mimic.

Workflow Tips: Prepare the recreation for complex intuitive. Reenact diverse fluids like nectar and water utilizing Thickness.

Smoke

Smoke recreations make practical fire, smoke, and fog impacts.

1. Including Smoke Material science

   - Select an protest.
   - In the Material science Properties, tap Liquid and set the Sort to Smoke.

2. Key Settings

   - Flow Sort: Select between Smoke, Fire, or Fire+Smoke.
   - Domain Settings: Alter determination, smoke thickness, and warm.

3. Workflow Tips

   - Use Versatile Space to optimize recreation space.
   - Combine smoke with Constrain Areas for energetic impacts.

Drive Areas

Oblige Ranges affect fabric science reenactments by counting qualities like gravity or wind.

1. Counting Drive Regions

- Press Move + A > Drive Field.
- Choose a sort (e.g., Wind, Vortex, Alluring).

2. Key Settings

- Strength: Characterizes the force's concentrated.
- Falloff: Controls the extend of affect.
- Noise: Includes intervention to the oblige.

3. Common Compel Ranges

- Wind: Reenacts directional wind.
- Turbulence: Incorporates chaotic development to particles and fluids.
- Vortex: Makes spiraling movement.

CHAPTER FOURTEEN

Animation & Rigging

Armatures

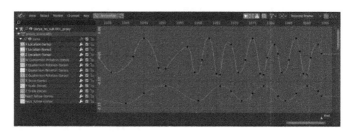

Armatures are the bones' skeletons to fix and invigorate objects - generally characters.

1. Making Armatures

- To include an armature, press Move + A > Armature > Single Bone,
- With the armature chosen press Tab to enter Alter Mode, making hence more bones,
- Press E to Expel bones and construct a skeleton structure.

2. Bone Chain of command

Child rearing Bones with a bone chosen, press Ctrl + P, hence child rearing bones for various leveled development.

Bone Roll: The N board in Alter Mode permits changes within the introduction of the bones.

1.Armature Modifiers

Apply the Armature Modifier to work objects to tie it to the skeleton. Within the Modifiers tab select as modifier's question the armature. Controls Weight Portray for each bone the impact on the work.

Shape Keys

Shape Keys are utilized for work miss happening, such as facial expressions or muscle advancements.

1. Counting Shape Keys

- Select a work and go to the Address Data Properties tab.

- Click on Shape Keys and press + to incorporate a Preface shape key (the default shape).

- Add another key for a specific miss happening (e.g., smile, frown, eyebrow raise).

2. Changing Shape Keys

- Switch to Change Mode to modify the geometry for each shape key.

- Present between the Preface and other shapes by utilizing the Slider open inside the Shape Keys board. Drivers can be utilized to drive the regard of shape keys with respect to other objects or parameters.

3. Enlivening Shape Keys: Keyframe the shape key values direct on the sliders. Smooth moves will require utilizing the F-Curve Editor for modifying inclusion between keyframes.

Imperatives

Constraints set limits to the behavior that can be connected to objects or bones, restricting their developments or activities.

A few of the foremost common sorts of limitations incorporate:

- Area, Revolution, Scale: Controls the development, revolution, or scaling of an question relative to others.

- Restrain: Obliges an object's development or revolution inside a indicated extend.

- Reverse Kinematics (IK): This permits control of a chain of bones from the tip, such as for quickening legs or arms.

- Track To: Makes an protest or bone track to a target protest. Valuable for eyes, cameras, etc.

- Copy: Duplicates changes from another protest.

Actions

Exercises are collections of keyframes that characterize how a specific challenge or settle moves over time.

1. Making Exercises

In Pose Mode, bones are vivified by selecting any bone and pressing I to implant keyframes characterizing its advancement in zone, transformation, or scale.

Take Action; all Exercises for an dissent are put absent inside the Dope Sheet underneath the Action Editor.

2. Supervising Exercises

Utilize the Action Editor to form some exercises for an challenge or settle; for event, walking, running, bouncing. It is conceivable to combine or blend various exercises together inside the NLA Editor for more complex liveliness.

NLA Editor (Non-Linear Activity Editor)

The NLA Editor is utilized to combine and oversee activities for more complex and nonlinear activitys of a protest.

1.Utilizing the NLA Editor : Open the NLA Editor from the Action Workspace. Each movement made inside the Activity Editor appears up as a Strip interior the NLA Editor. To incorporate a unused action, press the Pushed Down Movement button inside the Action Editor.

2.Mixing Exercises: The Blend In/Out properties are utilized to move effectively between each movement:

3. Mixing and Layering

- Use distinctive strips to layer energy, such as blending a walking action with an arm improvement.

- Adjust the weight and blending mode of each strip to fine-tune the blend.

Drivers

Drivers are utilized to control one property with another, permitting for complex natural and mechanization in energy.

1.Including Drivers

- Right-click on a property (e.g., region, shape key regard, texture color) and select Incorporate Driver.

- Go to the Chart Editor, switch to Drivers mode, and change the driver's parameters.

2.Driver Sorts

Single Property: Utilize the regard of another property as a driver; for case, controlling a door's turn based on a light heightened.

Custom Properties: Counting a custom property to an address - such as a slider that controls many viewpoints of a settle.

3.Driver Components: Including components to drivers licenses the client to characterize the relationship between the controlling and controlled properties.

Illustration: A custom property on an dissent driving the regard of a material's obnoxiousness.

CHAPTER FIFTEEN

Add-ons

Installing Add-ons

To present an add-on in Blender, take after these steps:

1. Download the Add-on

- Download the add-on from a trusted source:
- Blender's official location or community social occasions. Add-ons are commonly bundled as.zip records but can besides be individual.py (Python) scripts.

2. Introduce the Add-on

- Go to Alter > Inclinations > Add-ons tab.

- Press the Introduce button at the beat of the window. Browse to and select the downloaded.zip or.py record.

- Tap Introduce Add-on.

3. Enable the Add-on

- Once presented, the add-on will appear up inside the list underneath Add-ons.

- Check the box near to the add-on to enable it.

- A few add-ons have additional settings or choices that show up when the entry inside the list is amplified.

4. Managing Add-ons

- You'll cripple or clear add-ons anytime from the Slants window.

- For predominant execution, evade engaging pointless add-ons.

Official Add-ons

Blender as of now has a few inbuilt, official add-ons that contain awesome set of apparatuses and functionalities that amplify your workflow. A few of the critical official add-ons incorporate the taking after:

Fundamental Official Add-ons

1. Grease Pencil Apparatuses: The Grease Pencil add-on permits drawing 2D liveliness straightforwardly in 3D space. 2. Hub Wrangler: A very imperative add-on for those into working with Shades Hubs. Making it less demanding by giving a plenty of easy routes, it includes functionality to hubs, such as a straightforward interface framework for hubs or to appear nodes' yields consequently.

3. Unbending nature: The Unbending nature programmed add-on utilized to fix humanoid characters. You'll have an editable or imitable fix for something lovely fast.

4. FBX Import/Export: Official importer/exporter for FBX, current industry standard for all amusement advancement and liveliness pipelines.

5. UV Toolkit: An add-on which gives additional UV unwrapping apparatuses that streamline the method of laying out and altering UV maps of networks.

6. Activity Hubs: A procedural hub based framework to form complex activity, movement illustrations and visual impacts.

7. 2D Activity Instruments: These devices give a full extend of capacities for 2D movement pencil drawing, fixing of 2D characters, and quickening 2D shapes.

8. Import-Export Scripts : Official merchants and exporters for designs like OBJ, STL, 3DS, Collada, and others, encouraging information exchange between Blender and other 3D program.

Community Add-ons

Community add-ons are made by clients and originators outside of the official Blender Foundation. They allow a wide amplify of value, from advanced modeling rebellious to action utilities. A number of the community add-ons join:

1. Circle Devices: Circle Apparatuses may be a well known community add-on that increases Blender's work changing devices, giving unused disobedient for bridging circles, altering vertices, and more.

2.Difficult Ops / BoxCutter

• These increments are imperative to troublesome surface modeling, counting more advanced Boolean, cutting of systems, and procedural workflows.

3. Auto-Rig Proficient

• Usually regularly a compelling settling add-on that produces a distinction realize quick creation of humanoid and animal rigs with modified weighting and customizing the settle.

4. Mesh-machine

• Work Machine contains a set of advanced disobedient for work modeling, which joins smooth options, updating edge stream, and troublesome surface modeling disobedient.

5. Substance in Blender:

This add-on planning Substance Painter and Substance Planner specifically with Blender, giving a reliable workflow with respect to surface depict.

6. MiraTools

MiraTools may be a high-end modeling addon that gives an characteristic interface for box modeling and work modifying operations, checking beveling and poly gathering, among various others.

7. QuickRig

Quick Settle is an modified rigger for humanoid characters, sketched out to assist illustrators and character originators save time.

8. V-Ray for Blender

In the event that you're utilizing the V-Ray rendering engine, this is often often a community-created add-on that gives the desired support to facilitated V-Ray with Blender, publicizing advanced highlights in rendering.

9. Energy Layers

This add-on presents a layer-based workflow for development, engaging you to work in several development layers at the same time, comparative to working with layers in picture altering computer program.

10. Blender Publicize / Gumroad Add-ons

A parcel of designers offer or pass on their add-ons through third-party channels like Blender Grandstand and Gumroad. These has carry a couple of the finest community-developed add-ons, custom-made for specific needs or businesses.

Where to Find Add-ons

Blender Publicize: Commercial center for Blender-specific add-ons and assets.

Gumroad: Various designers offer paid or free add-ons there.

Blender Experts Gathering: Official Gathering where clients share their add-ons and scripts.

GitHub: Many makers pushed their free open-source add-ons in GitHub, and it licenses download and modifies with energize establishments.

www.ingramcontent.com/pod-product-compliance
Lightning Source LLC
Chambersburg PA
CBHW071004050326
40689CB00014B/3484